The Official
Celtic
Football Club
Annual 2009

Written by Joe Sullivan & David Friel

A Grange Publication

© 2008. Published by Grange Communications Ltd., Edinburgh, under licence from Celtic Football Club. Printed in the EU.

Photographs by Alan Whyte & Angus Johnson.
Celtic logo is a registered trademark of The Celtic Football Club.
ISBN 978-1-906211-30-1

£6.99

Contents

Club Honours

Scottish League Winners [42 times]

1892/93, 1893/94, 1895/96, 1897/98,
1904/05, 1905/06, 1906/07, 1907/08,
1908/09, 1909/10, 1913/14, 1914/15,
1915/16, 1916/17, 1918/19, 1921/22,
1925/26, 1935/36, 1937/38, 1953/54,
1965/66, 1966/67, 1967/68, 1968/69,
1969/70, 1970/71, 1971/72, 1972/73,
1973/74, 1976/77, 1978/79, 1980/81,
1981/82, 1985/86, 1987/88, 1997/98,
2000/01, 2001/02, 2003/04, 2005/06,
2006/07, 2007/08

Scottish Cup Winners [34 times]

1892, 1899, 1900, 1904, 1907, 1908,
1911, 1912, 1914, 1923, 1925, 1927,
1931, 1933, 1937, 1951, 1954, 1965,
1967, 1969, 1971, 1972, 1974, 1975,
1977, 1980, 1985, 1988, 1989, 1995,
2001, 2004, 2005, 2007

League Cup Winners [13 times]

1956/57, 1957/58, 1965/66, 1966/67,
1967/68, 1968/69, 1969/70, 1974/75,
1982/83, 1997/98, 1999/00, 2000/01,
2005/06

European Cup Winners 1967
Coronation Cup Winners 1953

Club Directory & Honours

Celtic Football Club
Celtic Park, Glasgow, G40 3RE

Telephone:
0871 226 1888

Website:
www.celticfc.net

Formed:
1888

Stadium:
Celtic Park

Capacity:
60,456

Home strip colours:
Green/white hooped shirts, white
shorts, white socks

Away strip colours:
Gold with green trim

Record attendance:
92,000 v Rangers, 1938

Record victory:
11-0 v Dundee, 1895

Record defeat:
0-8 v Motherwell, 1937

**Most league goals
in one season:**
50 - Jimmy McGrory, 1935/36

**Most Premier/SPL goals
in one season:**
35 - Brian McClair, 1986/87
35 - Henrik Larsson, 2000/01

Club Sponsors

Celtic plc Directors:

John Reid

Peter Lawwell

Eric Riley

Dermot Desmond

Tom Allison

Brian McBride

Brian Wilson

Ian Livingston

CFAC Directors:

Peter Lawwell

Eric Riley

John Keane

Michael McDonald

Kevin Sweeney

Manager:

Gordon Strachan

Assistant Manager:

Garry Pendrey

Coach:

Neil Lennon

Head of Youth:

Chris McCart

**Football Development
Manager:**

John Park

Reserve Coach:

Willie McStay

Youth Team Coach:

John McLaughlan

Club Doctor:

Derek McCormack

Kit Controller:

John Clark

CLYDESDALE BANK PREMIER LEAGUE FIXTURES 2008/09

DATE	TEAM
10/08/08	St Mirren (H)
17/08/08	Dundee United (A)
23/08/08	Falkirk (H)
31/08/08	Rangers (H)
13/09/08	Motherwell (A)
20/09/08	Kilmarnock (A)
27/09/08	Aberdeen (H)
04/10/08	Hamilton Accies (H)
18/10/08	Inverness CT (A)
25/10/08	Hibernian (H)
01/11/08	Hearts (A)
08/11/08	Motherwell (H)
12/11/08	Kilmarnock (H)
15/11/08	Hamilton Accies (A)
22/11/08	St Mirren (A)
29/11/08	Inverness CT (H)
06/12/08	Hibernian (A)
13/12/08	Hearts (H)
20/12/08	Falkirk (A)
27/12/08	Rangers (A)
03/01/09	Dundee United (H)
17/01/09	Aberdeen (A)
24/01/09	Hibernian (H)
31/01/09	Inverness CT (A)
14/02/09	Rangers (H)
21/02/09	Motherwell (A)
28/02/09	St Mirren (H)
04/03/09	Kilmarnock (A)
14/03/09	Falkirk (H)
21/03/09	Dundee United (H)
04/04/09	Hamilton Accies (H)
11/04/09	Hearts (A)
18/04/09	Aberdeen (H)

All fixtures are subject to change.
Post-split fixtures will be announced at a later date

Copyright © and Database Right The Scottish Premier League Limited 2008.

GORDON STRACHAN

Factfile:

D.O.B: 09/02/57

Born: Edinburgh, Scotland

Playing career record: Dundee (1974-77), Aberdeen (1977-84), Manchester United (1984-89), Leeds United (1989-95), Coventry City (1995-97)

Playing Honours: Scottish Championship 1980, 1984 / Scottish Cup 1982, 1983, 1984 / UEFA Cup-Winners' Cup 1983 / UEFA Super Cup 1983 / English FA Cup 1985 /, English Second Division (old) 1990, English First Division (Old) 1992, FA Charity Shield 1992

Managerial history: Coventry City (1996-2001), Southampton (2001-2004), Celtic (2005-present)

Managerial honours: Scottish Premier League Championship 2005/06, 2006/07, 2007/08 / Scottish League Cup 2005/06 / Scottish Cup 2006/07

50 Scotland caps and member of the SFA Hall of Fame

Scottish Football Writers' Player of the Year 1980

English Football Writers' Player of the Year 1991

Scottish Football Writers' Manager of the Year 2006 & 2007

Scottish PFA Manager of the Year 2007

FIFA/SOS Ambassador for Scotland

A TRIO of Scottish Premier League titles in his first three years at Celtic has secured Gordon Strachan status as one of the most successful managers in the club's history.

Only Celtic legends Jock Stein and Willie Maley have matched that three-in-a-row achievement and, when you add his domestic cup and European success, the current Hoops boss has an incredible record.

A quartet of new faces arrived at Celtic in the summer of 2007, with Scott McDonald, Chris Killen, Massimo Donati and Scott Brown bolstering a championship-winning squad.

The early signs were positive, with the new Bhoys helping Celtic into the group stages of the UEFA Champions League after a dramatic qualifying victory over Russian giants Spartak Moscow.

Into the UEFA Champions League proper, Celtic qualified for the last 16 for the second year running, from a group containing AC Milan, Benfica and Shakhtar Donetsk – finishing in second place.

In the next round, Celtic were drawn against Catalan aces Barcelona and were eventually edged out 4-2 on aggregate after two epic clashes.

On the domestic front, Celtic were locked in a tight battle with Rangers and faced a mighty test to retain their title as the season reached its final stages.

The Celtic manager strengthened his squad in January by bringing Andreas Hinkel, Ben Hutchinson, Koki Mizuno, Barry Robson and Georgios Samaras (on loan) to the club. Those players would play a crucial role in the run-in.

Trailing seven points in early April, the Hoops produced a Magnificent Seven successive wins to clinch the title on the last day of the season.

Dutch striker Jan Vennegoor of Hesselink scored the goal that ultimately won the league, while Aiden McGeady dominated the Player of the Year awards.

After three trophy-laden years at the club, Gordon Strachan has established Celtic as the dominant force in the Scottish game.

He has won every team, and personal, honour available over the last three years, but you can be certain he will have his eye on more success in season 2008/09.

WE'VE been here before haven't we! The Bhoys started their league campaign by raising the Championship flag before the opening game against Kilmarnock – but not before warm-up games in Switzerland and the USA as well as north and south of the border back home.

There was transfer activity as well with Massimo Donati and Chris Killen joining up with Scott McDonald and Scott Brown who had already signed pre-contracts with the Hoops.

Following the 0-0 opener with Killie, there were impressive wins over Falkirk (4-1), Aberdeen (3-1) and Hearts (5-0) but a 1-1 away draw with Spartak Moscow in the UEFA Champions League qualifier paved the way for one of the most remarkable European nights ever at Celtic Park.

Another 1-1 draw led to nail-biting extra-time and penalties where Artur Boruc saved Maxim Kalinichenko's effort and the now historic pile-on ensued – plus the Celts were through to the UEFA Champions League proper!

BEST BHOY
Artur Boruc
Spot-kick
Saviour

"IN 25 years' time, when I'm on the golf course somewhere, this game will come back to me. It was the European tie that had everything and what a good side Spartak Moscow turned out to be."

Gordon Strachan after the Spartak game.

SEPTEMBER

"Scott was fantastic and I couldn't believe it was his first ever hat-trick. I would have bet with anybody that he had scored three in a game before Saturday, but they were all good goals, and all from inside the six-yard box."

Gordon Strachan on Scott McDonald's hat-trick.

CELTIC'S UEFA Champions League Group D challenge could hardly have been any tougher as they shared the section with AC Milan, Benfica and Shakhtar Donetsk – all old foes of recent years. First though, there was SPL duty to be taken care of and St Mirren and Inverness CT were both hit for five as the Celts maintained their challenge for the title before their second early-season trip behind what used to be the Iron Curtain.

A 2-0 defeat in Ukraine as Shakhtar struck twice inside the first eight minutes wasn't the best of starts to the European campaign and that was quickly followed by a 3-2 defeat featuring a late goal for Hibs at Easter Road. The Hoops got back in the winning habit with a 2-1 League Cup victory over Dundee and were to finish the month on a real high against the other side from the City of Discovery when Scott McDonald rattled in a hat-trick against Dundee United – the first of his career!

OCTOBER

BEST BHOY
Stephen McManus
Captain's Role

THERE was no getting by the influence of Celtic's Aussie striker during this month either as he was to the fore in a couple of crucial victories that would have great bearing on two league tables – the SPL and the UEFA Champions League Group D.

In the first two games of the month, within days of each other, Scott McDonald hit last-minute winning goals against teams from opposite ends of the footballing spectrum – AC Milan and Gretna.

The Italian giants were the first to fall as a very soft penalty decision allowed Kaka to equalise Stephen McManus' opener but McDonald was on hand to pounce with the last-gasp winner.

He did the same four days later at Fir Park against the Premier new boys but defeats to Rangers, Benfica, with a late goal, and then Hearts in the League Cup couldn't take the shine off the month – and McDonald even hit another hat-trick, this time against Motherwell as the Celts finished October on top of the league.

"I think overall we deserved to beat AC Milan. We know how important it is to win your home matches in the Champions League and we did that. I didn't know much about the goal to be honest. I just saw the ball flash across the goal, I connected with it and the ball went in. That was all that matters."

Stephen McManus on his vital opening goal against AC Milan.

BEST BHOY
Massimo Donati
Last Action
Hero

THERE were only four games in November and not only did the Hoops record wins in each of them, in doing so they took their winning run in the UEFA Champions League to three successive victories over top-class opposition.

Not that the domestic opposition were proving to be any shrinking violets either but wins over Kilmarnock and Aberdeen maintained Celtic's defence of the title they had won for the two previous seasons.

Another two Scott McDonald goals saw off Kilmarnock 2-1 at Rugby Park while Aiden McGeady pounced just before the break to give Celtic a 1-0 win over Portuguese legends Benfica.

Aberdeen were next to fall 3-0 at Celtic Park as the Hoops prepared for the visit of Shakhtar Donetsk and, like Benfica, there was to be revenge for the away defeat.

The Ukrainians took an early lead but Jiri Jarosik levelled just before the break and, in the 92nd minute, Massimo Donati manufactured the winner.

"It was one of those nights I'll remember for the rest of my life. I'm delighted because I've waited a while for my first UEFA Champions League goal. I got a half-yard of space and it took a slight deflection but I will take anything at the minute. It's the biggest goal of my life."

Aiden McGeady on his UEFA Champions League winner against Benfica.

"For myself it's pleasing. There has only been one other Celtic captain who has taken the team to the last 16, and that was Neil Lennon last year. Personally, I'm proud of the achievement, but it's all been about the team and the way we've worked together. I'm just delighted with what we've done. We went to the San Siro to play the European champions and lost 1-0. But the most important thing is that we are into the last 16 of the UEFA Champions League. It is a fantastic achievement and the lads should all be proud."

Skipper Stephen McManus on qualifying for the UEFA Champions League last 16 for the second year in succession.

BY far the busiest month so far with no fewer than eight matches played and even a 1-0 defeat to AC Milan in Italy couldn't stop the Hoops qualifying for the UEFA Champions League last 16 for the second consecutive season.

There were mixed fortunes on the domestic front though as three 1-1 draws were played out against Hearts, St Mirren and Hibernian and an unexpected 3-2 defeat to Inverness CT also hindered the side, but the Bhoys still picked up important points.

Falkirk were beaten 4-0 thanks to an Aiden McGeady hat-trick while Dundee United were beaten 2-0 on Boxing Day and the Celts closed the year with a 3-0 win over Gretna.

Everything was put into perspective that very same evening, though, as news broke of Phil O'Donnell's tragic death following Motherwell's 5-3 win over Dundee United.

Scottish football went into mourning and, of course, the news hit Celtic Park with particular sadness as Phil played in the Hoops for five years.

BEST BHOY
Aiden McGeady
Treble
Topper

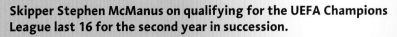

JANUARY

BEST BHOY
Scott Brown
Ever-present
so far

"Looking at the fixture list, we'll be playing two games a week a lot of the time. That's what I love. We'll be training Monday, Tuesday, playing on a Wednesday, training Thursday, Friday and the gaffer will maybe give us the Sunday off. That's perfect for me. There are still a lot of games to go this season and, in my opinion, the more you play the better you become. I'd rather we had this amount of games to be honest."

Scott Brown on the growing backlog of games.

SCOTTISH football, and Celtic and Motherwell in particular, started to come to terms with the sad loss of Phil O'Donnell and the Hoops played only three games during the first month of the year.

All three games were victories and the run started off with a home Scottish Cup win over Stirling Albion – a game in which new Bhoy, German defender Andreas Hinkel made his debut after joining from Seville.

The full-back wasn't to be the only addition during the January transfer window as he was joined by Barry Robson from Dundee United, Georgios Samaras on loan from Manchester City, Koki Mizuno from Japanese side JEF United and Ben Hutchinson from Middlesbrough.

The month finished with two tight 1-0 victories over Kilmarnock and Falkirk – but the Bhoys were still four points behind Rangers in the championship battle with both teams having played 22 games each.

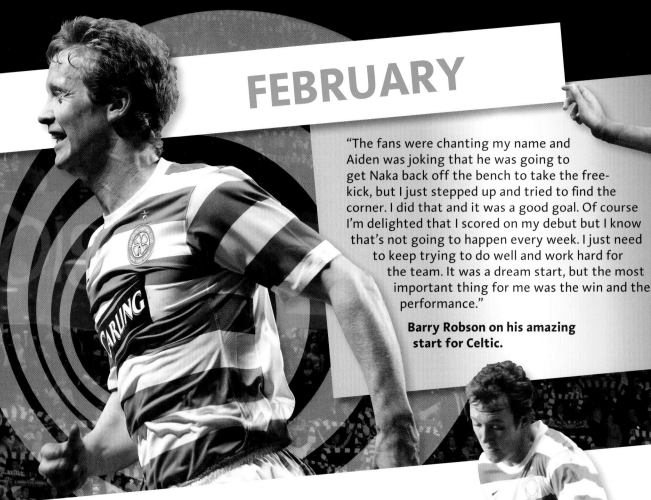

FEBRUARY

"The fans were chanting my name and Aiden was joking that he was going to get Naka back off the bench to take the free-kick, but I just stepped up and tried to find the corner. I did that and it was a good goal. Of course I'm delighted that I scored on my debut but I know that's not going to happen every week. I just need to keep trying to do well and work hard for the team. It was a dream start, but the most important thing for me was the win and the performance."

Barry Robson on his amazing start for Celtic.

THE Hoops got right back into the swing of things with five straight domestic wins – one in the Scottish Cup and four in the league – with a very slim loss to European giants Barcelona providing the only blip.

New Bhoy Georgios Samaras got off to a flier by coming off the bench to score on his debut in the 5-1 cup win over Kilmarnock but, the following week, Barry Robson was to go one better by having an even more extraordinary debut.

The Celts were 4-1 up against Aberdeen when Robson replaced Shunsuke Nakamura in the 73rd minute. The Hoops soon earned a free-kick which Robson swept into the net to become the first Celt to score with his first ever touch of the ball for the club.

Even that couldn't overshadow Aiden McGeady's drag-back shuffle preceding Scott McDonald's second goal of the day as the Celts clocked up two successive 5-1 away wins.

Hearts (3-0), St Mirren (1-0) and Inverness CT (2-1) were also defeated but despite twice taking the lead against Barca thanks to Jan Vennegoor of Hesselink and Barry Robson, the Celts were edged out 3-2 by the Catalans in the UEFA Champions League.

BEST BHOY
Aiden McGeady
No need
to ask

MARCH

THE end-of-month figures showed that the Celts were now six points behind Rangers with the Ibrox side also having a game in hand – and the Hoops had also been knocked out of the Scottish Cup by Aberdeen after a replay.

There was also a 1-0 defeat in Barcelona confirming the UEFA Champions League exit but the month got off to a flying start with a 2-0 win over Hibs – a team the Hoops had failed to beat in two earlier attempts that season.

Gretna also fell to their second successive 3-0 defeat to Celtic while there was also a 0-0 draw with Dundee United, but the main game was the final match of the month when the Hoops travelled to Ibrox knowing that a win would put them level on points – although Rangers still had that important game in hand.

The Celts lost the game 1-0, meaning they had a mountain to climb with, possibly, a nine-point gap to make up and time running out as the season started to enter its final phase – but there was also the great news that Neil Lennon had returned in a coaching capacity.

"It's going to be very hard for us to win the league - but it's possible. We need to win every game now and it's possible that we can do that. I definitely have the players here who are capable of winning those eight games. When we're on form, our strikers have scored enough goals and we need to make sure we keep clean sheets. With the system of the SPL split, we're up against the best teams in the league and that's the same the other way with Rangers. We're just working on the assumption that we need to win every game and we'll take it from there. "

Gordon Strachan following that Ibrox defeat.

BEST BHOY
Jan Vennegoor
of Hesselink
Goal Getter

APRIL

BEST BHOY
Shunsuke
Nakamura
Goal of
the Season

WE all knew that Celtic had to win their remaining eight games while hoping that Rangers would slip and we knew that would be hard – what we didn't expect was that, in the very first of those matches, Motherwell would visit Celtic Park and win 1-0!

Amazingly though, if those two successive defeats dented morale at Celtic Park you would never have noticed it.

The following weekend, the roles were reversed as Motherwell played host to Celtic and the Bhoys came away with a vital 4-1 win – every game from now on in was vital – and Rangers were next on the agenda three days later.

It was a night to remember as an absolute screamer from Shunsuke Nakamura and a last-minute clincher from Jan Vennegoor of Hesselink sealed the win before a crucial Georgios Samaras goal clinched all three points against Aberdeen at the weekend – and then Aiden McGeady picked up both the Player and Young Player of the Year awards at the PFA ceremony.

Next up were Rangers again and advantage swayed from one team to the other before a Barry Robson penalty in the 70th minute complemented Scott McDonald's earlier double beautifully in a 3-2 win – quite a good month was April.

"Winning the game was all that mattered but, yes, from a personal point of view it was nice to get a couple of goals. They have not been coming as frequently for me lately and I've been a little frustrated by that. But I have been working hard and when you score it gives you a massive lift. It was great to get the monkey off my back and score my first goals in a Celtic strip against Rangers, but this win will be significant only if we win our next three games and Rangers drop points."

Scott McDonald after scoring a double against Rangers.

MAY

BEST BHOYS
The Squad
Championship
Celts

IF April was good, then May was going to get a whole lot better, but the success was tinged with sadness when Celtic legend Tommy Burns passed away midway through the month.

The outpouring of grief wasn't limited to the confines of Celtic Park as Scottish football paid homage to a man who was Celtic to the core and no-one would have been more pleased than Tommy about the way Celtic's season ended.

The month started with a 2-1 away win over Motherwell, with Scott McDonald and Georgios Samaras netting after the home side had taken the lead, and that was followed up with a 2-0 win over Hibernian while the Celts had to wait 11 days before playing Dundee United in the final game of the season.

Rangers, meanwhile, had dropped points to Hibs and Motherwell in drawn games so, despite wins over Motherwell, Dundee United and St Mirren, the league race was blown wide open.

Both sides went into the final day level on points with the Celts having a better goal-difference of four, but while the Ibrox side went 2-0 down at Pittodrie, a Jan Vennegoor of Hesselink header sealed the points and the Championship at Tannadice.

"It goes without saying that it was an awesome feeling to lift my first trophy as captain. Words can't explain the emotions running through my mind as I stepped up to lift the championship trophy – it was a special moment. I've enjoyed so many fantastic occasions since breaking into the Celtic first-team but, without a doubt, that was the major highlight. To captain your boyhood heroes to the title on the final day of the season is the stuff dreams are made of."

Stephen McManus relives the glory.

SPOT THE DIFFERENCE

There are 12 differences between the double take of this picture featuring Aiden McGeady taking on Shakhtar Donetsk, the first one has been circled, now see if you can spot the rest. Answers on pages 60/61.

At the end of a long hard season, Scott Brown reaches for the sky at Tannadice, but how much do you know about the rest of the 2007/08 championship?

SPL SEASON 2007/08 CHAMPIONSHIP QUIZ

QUESTIONS

01	Against which club did the Hoops raise the league flag?
02	Who scored the opening goal of Celtic's campaign?
03	Which club did the Bhoys face for the first time ever during the term?
04	Which two Celts scored the first hat-tricks of their careers that season?
05	How many times did Celtic score five goals during the championship?
06	How many clean sheets did Celtic record?
07	And how many times did the Bhoys fail to score?
08	How many players did Celtic use during the campaign?
09	Which player made the most appearances?
10	Aside from new signings, which four Celts made their debuts that season?

How did you do? Find out with the answers on pages 60/61.

Did you know...

When Celt Joe Craig came on as a sub for Scotland against Sweden in 1977, he scored with his first touch – and as it was a header, he became the first player to score for Scotland before he actually kicked the ball!

HAVE you ever wondered what the Bhoys get up to before a game? Well we have the answers right here in your Celtic Annual.

We have NINE pre-match rituals that some of your favourites just HAVE to go through and there are also NINE tasty tit-bits to help you choose your perfect pre-match meal.

It doesn't end there though – we have some magnificent top training tips from the pros at the Celtic Academy for NINE vital skills.

Find out the rest of the nine-in-a-rows on pages 38/39 and 44/45.

CELTS' SUPERSTITIONS

The Bhoys' pre-match rituals that are strictly adhered to:

SCOTT BROWN

I don't really have a specific pre-match routine or anything, but I have had the same shin-guards for seven years and I won't change them until I have to.

GARY CALDWELL

I always change my entire kit at half-time in a game – socks, shorts, t-shirt, strip…everything. It sends Clarky and Joe (Celtic kitmen) mad, but it's just something I like to do.

PAUL CADDIS

The only superstition I have is that I always put on my left shin-guard first, followed by my right shin-guard. Then I put on my left boot first, followed by my right boot.

FOOD FOR THOUGHT

The players' scran-plan before the action starts:

JAN VENNEGOOR OF HESSELINK

I always have some Spaghetti Bolognese before games, because I feel that prepares me in the right way and sets me up for 90 minutes.

SCOTT BROWN

A lot of the boys eat chicken, pasta or rice, but I just prefer to have two bowls of Coco Pops – before every game that's what I eat.

GARY CALDWELL

I always have a bowl of cereal and then follow that up with some scrambled eggs on toast. It has to be a light meal before the game.

TOP TIPS

DRIBBLING

• To become a good dribbler, use the outside and inside of both feet. This helps you to keep the ball away from your opponent.

• Touch the ball with each step you take. This will create good control and increase your dribbling speed with the ball.

• Keep the ball close to you. This makes it easier to evade defenders when they try to tackle.

• Change the pace of your run. Sometimes it's better to slow down and then burst past your opponent at speed.

• Running towards an opponent at speed also puts them under pressure and increases the chance of them making a mistake!

• Keep your head up so you know if someone is making a run, another defender is approaching, or there is space to attack.

• Improve your weak foot by practicing. If you continue to strike the ball against a wall with your bad foot, you will see improvement.

• Use your body to protect and shield the ball from opponents.

• Try to keep the ball on the foot that is furthest from the defender – so that you can protect the ball.

• One of the best ways to improve dribbling is to practice with a tennis ball. That will make dribbling a full-sized football much easier.

PASSING

• When learning to pass the ball, start off by using the inside of the foot and then start using the outside when you feel more confident.

• Always make sure there is enough weight on the pass to reach the target.

• To find the target with pace and accuracy, point your standing foot towards the target and strike through the ball.

• The timing of the pass has to be correct and you must always be ready to receive the ball back – be on your toes and communicate at all times.

• When you're happy with your passing accuracy, start practicing with your weaker foot.

• Try to practice your passing on a daily basis and always be patient – practice will bring success.

HEADING

• Keep your eye on the ball as it comes towards you and use the centre of the forehead to make contact with the ball.

• For attacking headers, use your arms to generate lift for your jump and use the neck to assist in directing the ball.

• When heading towards goal, try to get in front of the defender and get above the ball to direct headers downwards.

• For defensive headers, generate power through the legs and step into/ through the ball.

• When clearing the ball under pressure, length and height are the key. You want to get the ball as far away from the danger area as possible.

• Try to avoid stationary jumping. Instead, leap off one foot and make connection with the ball at the highest point.

A WEEK IN THE LIFE OF STEPHEN McMANUS

They say a week is a long time in football but most of us would settle for just a day as a Celtic player. So what's it like to be the captain of the Hoops? Here, Stephen McManus takes us through a typical (if there is such a thing) week in the life of a Celt.

SUNDAY

Most of our away games are televised, so very often we have a match on a Sunday. I normally get up around 9am and have some toast for breakfast in the hotel. If it's a 2pm kick-off, we have our pre-match meal at 11 o'clock. I always have cereal and some chicken with pasta. The team bus leaves the hotel at 12.15pm and I listen to some of my favourite music on my iPod, before going out for the warm-up. After the game, I normally go home, have some dinner and rest up.

MONDAY

It's back into training at 11am for a cool-down session. In the past few years, we've had a lot of midweek European games at home, so the manager normally goes through some DVDs of the opposition with the team after training as well.

After some lunch and gym-work, I'll head back home for some rest and watch a film. In the afternoon, we sometimes do signing sessions at the Celtic Superstore, while I also try to answer some mail from supporters before getting to bed early.

TUESDAY

The day before the big European match, we normally train at Lennoxtown in the morning. It won't be a heavy session, just some ball work and finishing. Some of the boys then have a massage to make sure they are loosened off.

We all take our turns to do the press and I'll sometimes do it before the European matches. We speak to the broadcast and print press separately and it can take about 30 minutes.

After the press conference, we head to the team hotel and the boys have different routines. I just listen to music and watch DVDs before going for dinner and a sleep.

WEDNESDAY

The day of the match and we normally have some light breakfast followed by a training session. The manager will work on the shape of the team and we will do a lot of set-piece drills.

After training, it's back to the hotel for lunch and a sleep. We'll then have our pre-match meal at 4.30pm - it's chicken again for me - before leaving for Celtic Park at 6.15pm. The European games always start at 7.45pm, and afterwards we head through the mixed zone to speak to the media about the game. After that, there is sometimes time for a little celebration, but nothing too major because we always have a game at the weekend.

THURSDAY

It's into training early for another cool-down session with the boys who played. The other first-team squad members might do a bit extra. If any of the players have picked up knocks, they will also go to see the doctor and the physios.

After training, the manager will go over some things from the night before, and then we turn our attention to the game at the weekend. Your body always needs a lot of rest after big European games, so after catching up with the family, it's another early night for me.

FRIDAY

It's the day before another big match at home and we're in at the Lennoxtown Training Centre to prepare. Training consists of a variety of exercises and we finish with some shooting.
It's the Old Boys versus the Young Boys. At 25, I'm in-between but I'm somehow classed as an Old Boy. We normally win though!
After the press conference, the boys head home to get some rest before the match. I usually watch a DVD and get an early night.

SATURDAY

Match-day starts with some breakfast and we then meet at the stadium to go to the hotel for the pre-match meal. I again have chicken and pasta.
After the meal, the manager will name the team and go through the set-pieces again. It's then back on the bus to the stadium and I listen to my iPod for the journey.
We go out for the warm-up about half two. After the game, I'll spend a bit of time meeting the fans inside the stadium and signing autographs outside.
There is often a supporters' function to go to and if there is time, I sometimes head out for dinner on a Saturday night as well - hopefully to celebrate a successful week.

MAZE

The ball has to get from Artur Boruc in goal to Jan Vennegoor of Hesselink at the other end of the pitch so that he can score the goal that wins the Championship. Can you help it get there?

Find out how the ball got there on pages 60/61.

QUIZ QUESTIONS

01   How many times have Celtic won the league?

02   Which Celt made his debut against Stirling Albion in the Scottish Cup?

03   Can you name the Bhoy who also scored on his debut in the Scottish Cup against Kilmarnock?

04   How many times did Celtic play at Fir Park last season?

05   How many Celtic managers have led the team to three-in-a-row?

Check out the answers on pages 60/61.

WORDSEARCH

CLUES

01   Where to train the Celtic way.

02   The ground where the 2007/08 Championship was won.

03   Celtic's top marksman last season.

04   Heavenly name for Celtic Park.

05   Where Gordon Strachan used to manage Scott McDonald.

06   Jan Vennegoor of Hesselink's national team.

07   What Celtic have been for the past three seasons.

08   The man who managed Celtic to nine-in-a-row.

09   Celtic's pre-match ritual.

10   The Bhoys were the first British team to lift this trophy.

Answers on pages 60/61.

K	R	N	N	Y	K	R	M	C	E	Z	N	C
S	P	R	I	D	X	Z	M	C	L	E	W	E
O	N	A	R	E	V	N	I	K	T	D	O	L
U	T	L	R	B	T	D	J	H	F	Z	T	D
T	R	P	N	A	A	S	E	T	J	N	X	D
H	R	L	B	N	D	R	K	D	K	H	O	U
A	N	X	N	T	L	I	L	C	K	L	N	H
M	L	A	G	A	R	M	S	X	O	J	N	E
P	T	Z	N	R	B	N	C	E	H	J	E	H
T	T	D	J	T	W	V	L	Y	V	Y	L	T
O	S	N	O	I	P	M	A	H	C	T	L	V
N	P	U	C	N	A	E	P	O	R	U	E	H
S	C	O	T	T	M	C	D	O	N	A	L	D

Did you know...

No fewer than three Celts have scored hat-tricks on their debuts – Davie McLean 1907 (v Port Glasgow (h) 5-0), Tommy McInally 1919 (v Clydebank (h) 3-1) and Davie Prentice 1929 (v Raith Rovers (a) 4-1). The hat-trick of hat-tricks were all scored in league games.

THE CELTIC FOOTBALL CLUB
1888
celticfc.net
HOME
NEWS
TICKETS
Fixtures | Players | Community & Coaching | Charity Fund | Pools | About |

Artur Boruc

Position: Goalkeeper
Squad Number: 1
D.O.B: 20/02/80
Born: Siedlce, Poland
Height: 6'4"
Signed: 14/07/05 (loan)
17/10/05 (signed)
Debut: v Artmedia Bratislava (h)
4-0 (UCL) 02/08/05
Previous Clubs: Legia Warsaw, Dolcan Zabki (loan), Pogon Siedlce

Lee Naylor

Position: Left-back
Squad Number: 3
D.O.B: 19/03/80
Born: Walsall, England
Height: 5'10"
Signed: 25/08/06
Debut: v Hibernian (h) 2-1
(SPL) 26/08/06
Previous Clubs:
Wolverhampton Wanderers

Gary Caldwell

Position: Centre-back
Squad Number: 5
D.O.B: 12/04/82
Born: Stirling, Scotland
Height: 5'11"
Signed: 01/06/06
Debut: v Kilmarnock (h) 4-1
(SPL) 29/07/06
Previous Clubs: Hibernian, Derby County (loan), Coventry City (loan), Hibernian (loan), Darlington (loan), Newcastle United

PARADISE PROFILES

Search Celticfc.net [   ] GO

HOSPITALITY   SHOPPING

Sponsors | Corporate | celticfcbet | Finance | I Want To

Stephen McManus

Position: Centre-back
Squad Number: 4
D.O.B: 10/09/82
Born: Lanark, Scotland
Height: 6'2"
Signed: 20/08/99
Debut: v Hibernian (a) 4-0
(SPL) 21/03/04
Previous Clubs: Celtic Youth

Scott Brown

Position: Midfielder
Squad Number: 8
D.O.B: 25/06/85
Born: Hill o' Beath, Scotland
Height: 5'10"
Signed: 01/07/07
Debut: v Kilmarnock (h) 0-0
(SPL) 05/08/07
Previous Clubs: Hibernian

Andreas Hinkel

Position: Right-back
Squad Number: 2
D.O.B: 26/03/82
Born: Backnang, Germany
Height: 6'0"
Signed: 04/01/08
Debut: v Stirling Albion (h)
3-1 (SC) 12/01/08
Previous Clubs: Seville, VfB
Stuttgart

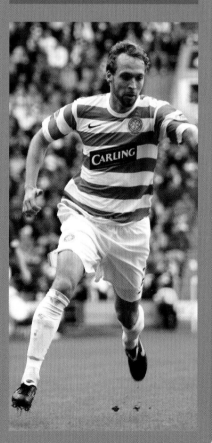

celticfc.net

Jan Vennegoor of Hesselink

Position: Centre-forward
Squad Number: 10
D.O.B: 07/11/78
Born: Oldenzaal, Netherlands
Height: 6'3"
Signed: 25/08/06
Debut: v Hibernian (h) 2-1
(SPL) 26/08/06
Previous Clubs: PSV
Eindhoven, FC Twente

Paul Hartley

Position: Midfielder
Squad Number: 11
D.O.B: 19/10/76
Born: Glasgow, Scotland
Height: 5'8"
Signed: 31/01/07
Debut: v Livingston (a) 4-1
(SC) 04/02/07
Previous Clubs: Hearts,
St Johnstone, Hibernian,
Raith Rovers, Millwall,
Hamilton

Barry Robson

Position: Midfielder
Squad Number: 19
D.O.B: 07/11/78
Born: Aberdeen, Scotland
Height: 5'11"
Signed: 31/01/08
Debut: v Aberdeen (a) 5-1
(SPL) 10/02/08
Previous Clubs: Dundee
United, Forfar Athletic
(loan), Inverness CT, Rangers

PARADISE PROFILES

Search Celticfc.net [ ] GO

HOSPITALITY | SHOPPING

Sponsors | Corporate | celticfcbet | Finance | I Want To

Koki Mizuno

Position: Winger
Squad Number: 29
D.O.B: 06/09/85
Born: Shimiz-Ku, Japan
Height: 5'8"
Signed: 31/01/08
Debut: N/A
Previous Clubs: JEF United

Darren O'Dea

Position: Defender
Squad Number: 48
D.O.B: 04/02/87
Born: Dublin, Ireland
Height: 6'1"
Signed: 01/08/05
Debut: v St Mirren (h) 2-0
(SLC) 19/09/06
Previous Clubs: Celtic Youth

Mark Wilson

Position: Full-back
Squad Number: 12
D.O.B: 05/06/84
Born: Glasgow, Scotland
Height: 5'10"
Signed: 16/01/06
Debut: v Dundee United (h)
3-3 (SPL) 28/01/06
Previous Clubs: Dundee
United

celticfc.net

HOME | NEWS | TICKETS

Fixtures | Players | Community & Coaching | Charity Fund | Pools | About | Fa

Evander Sno

Position: Centre-midfield
Squad Number: 15
D.O.B: 09/04/87
Born: Dordrecht,
Netherlands
Height: 6'1"
Signed: 21/06/06
Debut: v Kilmarnock
(h) 4-1 (SPL) 29/07/06
Previous Clubs: Feyenoord,
NAC Breda (loan), Ajax

Mark Brown

Position: Goalkeeper
Squad Number: 21
D.O.B: 28/02/81
Born: Motherwell, Scotland
Height: 6'1"
Signed: 18/01/07
Debut: v Hibernian (a) 1-2
(SPL) 20/05/07
Previous Clubs: Inverness CT,
Motherwell, Rangers

Thomas Gravesen

Position: Midfielder
Squad Number: 16
D.O.B: 11/03/76
Born: Vejle, Denmark
Height: 5'10"
Signed: 30/08/06
Debut: v Aberdeen (a) 1-0
(SPL) 09/09/06
Previous Clubs: Real Madrid,
Everton, Hamburger SV,
Vejle

PARADISE PROFILES

Search Celticfc.net [   ] GO

| HOSPITALITY | SHOPPING |

Sponsors | Corporate | celticfcbet | Finance | I Want To

Jean-Joel Perrier-Doumbe

Position: Full-back
Squad Number: 24
D.O.B: 27/09/78
Born: Paris, France
Height: 5'10"
Signed: 25/01/07
Debut: v Hearts (h) 1-3 (SPL)
29/04/07
Previous Clubs: Rennes,
Auxerre

Aiden McGeady

Position: Midfielder
Squad Number: 46
D.O.B: 04/04/86
Born: Glasgow, Scotland
Height: 5'10"
Signed: 20/07/02
Debut: v Hearts (a) 1-1 (SPL)
25/04/04
Previous Clubs: Celtic Youth

Shunsuke Nakamura

Position: Midfielder
Squad Number: 25
D.O.B: 24/06/78
Born: Kanagawa, Japan
Height: 5'10"
Signed: 29/07/05
Debut: v Dundee United (h)
2-0 (SPL) 06/08/05
Previous Clubs: Reggina,
Yokohama F Marinos

celticfc.net

HOME | **NEWS** | **TICKETS**

Fixtures | Players | Community & Coaching | Charity Fund | Pools | About | Fa

Massimo Donati

Position: Midfield
Squad Number: 18
D.O.B: 26/03/81
Born: Sedegliano, Italy
Height: 6'1"
Signed: 29/06/07
Debut: v Kilmarnock (h) 0-0 (SPL) 05/08/07
Previous Clubs: AC Milan, Atalanta (loan), Messina (loan), Sampdoria (loan), Torino (loan), Parma (loan)

Scott McDonald

Position: Centre-forward
Squad Number: 7
D.O.B: 21/08/83
Born: Melbourne, Australia
Height: 5'8"
Signed: 01/07/07
Debut: v Spartak Moscow (a) 1-1 (UCL) 15/08/07
Previous Clubs: Motherwell, Milton Keynes Dons (loan), Bournemouth (loan), Huddersfield (loan), Southampton

Ben Hutchinson

Position: Centre-forward
Squad Number: 23
D.O.B: 27/11/87
Born: Nottingham, England
Height: 5'11"
Signed: 31/01/08
Debut: v Hearts (h) 3-0 (SPL) 16/02/08
Previous Clubs: Middlesbrough

Search Celticfc.net [   ] GO

HOSPITALITY   SHOPPING

Sponsors | Corporate | celticfcbet | Finance | I Want To

Georgios Samaras

Position: Centre-forward
Squad Number: 9
D.O.B: 21/02/85
Born: Heraklion, Greece
Height: 6'4"
Signed: 29/01/08
Debut: v Kilmarnock (a) 5-1
(SC) 02/02/08
Previous Clubs: Manchester
City, Heerenveen

John Kennedy

Position: Centre-back
Squad Number: 41
D.O.B: 18/08/83
Born: Bellshill, Scotland
Height: 6'2"
Signed: 20/08/99
Debut: v Hibernian (a) 4-0
(SPL) 21/03/04
Previous Clubs: Celtic Youth

Cillian Sheridan

Position: Centre-forward
Squad Number: 26
D.O.B: 23/02/89
Born: Cavan, Ireland
Height: 6'2"
Signed: 10/02/06
Debut:v Inverness (a) 2-1
(SC) 25/02/07
Previous Clubs: Celtic Youth

HOME	NEWS	TICKETS

Fixtures | Players | Community & Coaching | Charity Fund | Pools | About | Fa

Derek Riordan

Position: Forward
Squad Number: 14
D.O.B: 16/01/83
Born: Edinburgh, Scotland
Height: 5'10"
Signed: 23/06/06
Debut: v Kilmarnock (h) 4-1
(SPL) 29/07/06
Previous Clubs: Hibernian

Chris Killen

Position: Striker
Squad Number: 33
D.O.B: 08/10/81
Born: Wellington, New
Zealand
Height: 6'
Signed: 02/06/07
Debut: v Kilmarnock (h) 0-0
(SPL) 05/08/07
Previous Clubs: Hibernian,
Oldham, Port Vale (loan),
Wrexham (loan), Man City

Paddy McCourt

Position: Winger
Squad Number: 20
D.O.B: 16/12/83
Born: Derry, Ireland
Height: 5'11"
Signed: 19/06/08
Debut: N/A
Previous Clubs: Rochdale,
Shamrock Rovers,
Derry City

PARADISE IN TANNADICE

PREMIER LEAGUE CHAMPIONS 07-08

Part Two of our inside story on what keeps the Celts on their toes – before and during a match.

CELTS' SUPERSTITIONS

The Bhoys' pre-match rituals that are strictly adhered to:

JOHN KENNEDY

When I start a game, I run away after we've done the huddle and jump into the air. That's the only superstition I have.

BARRY ROBSON

I don't really believe in superstitions, but I have had the same shin-guards for as long as I can remember. They have seen better days, but I'm not going to change them.

MARK WILSON

I'm not the superstitious type of guy, so I just get on with things and focus on the football – rather than superstitions.

FOOD FOR THOUGHT

The players' scran-plan before the action starts:

PAUL CADDIS

I always have chicken and rice soup before the game. I sometimes change, but that's my normal choice.

JOHN KENNEDY

I have some cornflakes, followed by toast with egg, normally scrambled. That keeps me going before the match.

BARRY ROBSON

There's nothing fancy about my pre-match meal – it's scrambled eggs and toast all the way. That's perfect for me.

TOP TIPS

PENALTIES

• There is no set way to take a penalty kick. A good penalty is one that hits the back of net.

• Make sure you hit the target and never change your mind during your run-up. If you plan to hit the bottom corner, aim for that area.

• Always be confident and composed. If you strike the ball well, the chances are that you will score.

• Practice your penalties by putting a marker at the area you are targeting. Keep trying to hit the marker and make sure there is pace and power on the ball.

• Don't try to be too clever. Chipped penalties look good, but most top professionals just pick a spot and make sure they strike the ball as cleanly as possible.

CORNERS

• It helps to pick a spot in the box and try to whip the ball as fast as you can towards that area. This gives your team-mates a better chance of attacking the ball.

• Goalkeepers tend to deal easily with corners that float into the box. To cause them problems, get as much pace/power and swerve on your corner as possible.

• Vary the style of corners. If you've fired two corners towards the back post, try and send one to the front post the next time. Let your team-mates know your intentions.

• If you are having a difficult time with your corners during a game, don't give up. One good delivery can make all the difference in a game!

• Practice your corners in training every day. That will help you when you get into a game situation.

SHOOTING

• Always remember that technique is more important than power. Stay composed when shooting.

• The first aim is to hit the target and at least make the goalkeeper save your shot.

• To hit a driven shot use the laces of your boot. That will give you more power.

• To place a shot in the corner, use the inside/outside of the boot. Practice this every day.

• Aim for the bottom corners of the goals in training. There is a greater success rate of scoring.

• Keep your body weight over the ball, not behind it. Don't lean back, or the ball will probably end up over the bar.

GHIRL POWER

THIS is a first for your Celtic Annual - but what a brilliant first it is as Celtic Ladies have gone from strength to strength in their inaugural season.

Since being launched at the start of the 2007/08 season, the Ghirls have made their presence known at all levels – from Under-11 up to the first team…

And the top team had a fantastic debut season, coming third in the Women's Premier League and losing out narrowly to traditional high flyers Hibernian by 3-1 after extra time in the Scottish Cup final.

There is no reserve league in women's football but that didn't stop Celtic Ladies from adding another feather to their cap as the Ghirls' reserve side entered the Second Division and promptly won the title, dropping only five points along the way, and gained promotion to the First Division thanks to amazing results of 6-2 and 9-0 against their closest league rivals, Maryhill and Tynecastle.

The Under-17s also finished third in the West-South-West League but ended their season on a real high by beating Hamilton Accies 3-2 on penalties in the final of the League Cup.

More silverware was popped in the bag by the Under-15s who very narrowly missed out on the Treble.

In the Central/West League they finished unbeaten as Champions and lifted the League Cup thanks to a 1-0 win over Falkirk, but there was to be heartbreak in the Scottish Youth Cup final.

Hibernian equalised with almost the last kick of the ball and, after extra-time, 24 penalty kicks were taken before Hibs edged it.

The Under-13s did go all the way though and lifted a glorious Treble in their first year of existence.

They were also unbeaten in the league and beat Clyde Cumbernauld 1-0 in the Scottish Cup final before hammering Paisley Saints 9-0 in the League Cup final.

The Under-11s take part in a non-competitive league and several of last season's players will already have moved up a grade.

Check out the Celtic Player Pathway to find out where it could lead you.

To find out more about Celtic Ladies and the training programmes contact Karen on: 0141 551 4332 – 9am to 5pm (Mon to Fri) email kmcinally@celticfc.co.uk

The Player Pathway for Girls and Women

Celtic LFC
playing in the
Scottish Women's Premier League
↑
Celtic LFC Reserves
↑
Girls' under 17
↑
Girls' under 15
↑
Girls' under 13
↑
Girls' under 11

Celtic Girls' Youth Academy

Centre of Excellence
↑
Development
under 8 to under 12
↑
Foundation
age 5 to under 7

Celtic Girls' Community Academy

GOLD TOP CELTS

A shirt story on the unveiling of Celtic's current change strip

THE new Celtic kits for this season were launched by Nike and the club at the start of the term backed with some striking imagery.

And the new change kit in particular featuring a stunning gold top, was the perfect colour for the SPL champions, who lifted a third successive title on a dramatic last day of the season.

The kit uses Nike Sphere Dry fabric technology, first used by Nike in national team kits worn in the 2006 World Cup.

This technology is designed to enhance player performance by wicking sweat through the material and away from the skin.

The fabric has a three-dimensional design with raised nodes on the underside that lift it away from the players' bodies to reduce 'cling' and allow air to circulate, assisting the body's own natural evaporation process.

On the inside collar of the shirt are the words: "It's not the creed nor nationality that counts. It's the man himself."

This is a quote from legendary manager Willie Maley that proudly demonstrates Celtic as a club open to all.

The third and final part of your Celtic annual's nifty nine.

CELTS' SUPERSTITIONS

The Bhoys' pre-match rituals that are strictly adhered to:

STEPHEN McMANUS

I sometimes listen to the same music on my iPod before a game and I always put my left shin-guard on before my right. It's just a routine I've followed for years.

DARREN O'DEA

It would take all day for me to list my superstitions. Everything I do in the lead-up to the game is a superstition. It's all done in a set way, for superstitious reasons. You wouldn't believe half the stuff I do.

NEIL LENNON

I was never too big on superstitions but I did have a specific pre-match routine and I always made sure my top was the last thing I put on before kick-off.

FOOD FOR THOUGHT

The players' scran-plan before the action starts:

MARK WILSON

I pretty much eat the same as the rest of the boys. I start off with cereal and finish off with scrambled eggs.

STEPHEN McMANUS

I have cereal, followed by chicken and pasta, or chicken and rice. I sometimes have toast as well.

DARREN O'DEA

I just stick to the normal pre-match meal for most football players – cereal followed by eggs on toast. It seems to work.

TOP TIPS

CONTROL

• Depending on how it arrives, use the inside, outside, top or bottom of the foot to control the ball.

• A skilful first touch gives a player time and space in which to move with the ball or find the best pass. Never let the ball run away from you.

• The chest is often required to bring the ball under control from awkward heights. Always try to move the ball into space to make a pass.

• The chest can also be used to pass the ball. Make sure you get enough power on the ball.

• Thigh control is required when the ball arrives at heights above the knee, but too low to head or chest down.

• The key of controlling the ball this way is to withdraw the thigh on impact to cushion it.

• Juggling the ball is a great way to improve thigh control. This will increase your touch.

• To control the ball with your head, make contact in the centre of your forehead, and use your whole body as a shock absorber to cushion the ball.

• When controlling with your head, make sure you bend your knees to drop your upper body and arch your back on impact.

• Your head must also be upwards when you receive the ball, in order to cushion it.

DIRECT FREE-KICKS

• Free-kick experts like Shunsuke Nakamura improve their natural ability through constant practice.

• Start off by hitting free-kicks from 18 yards. Gradually move the ball back when you feel more confident.

• Power is vital with free-kicks. Your direction might be perfect, but if there is not enough power on the ball, the goalkeeper will save the shot.

• When you are happy with the power on your free-kicks, start practicing putting some swerve and curl on the ball.

• Vary your style of free-kicks so that goalkeepers never know what to expect – go for the right and left sides of the goal, and vary the power and height.

CROSSING

• Approach the ball with confidence and get your cross in early.

• Always try to keep the cross away from the goalkeeper and focus on picking out a team-mate.

• Look up before you strike the cross and put your foot under the ball to get height on it.

• Practice crossing to the near post and back post from a wide area.

• Practice crossing from the bye-line across the goalkeeper, and to the back post.

• You can also practice disguising your cross by cutting the ball back to the edge of the box.

• Use both feet. Practice crossing from both wings using your left foot and right foot.

• Practice crossing the ball first-time, without taking a first touch, then practice crossing after taking a touch.

COLOUR ME IN

German defender Andreas Hinkel is on full alert here and we want you to get out your crayons, ink markers or paints and bring this empty image to full Celtic technicolour.

GUESS WHO?

1

2

3

4

5

6

Did you know...

Celtic's first ever trophy was won at Clyde's Barrowfield Park when the new Parkhead club beat Cowlairs 6-1 in the city's North Eastern Cup and they retained the trophy the following year before outgrowing the local competition.

THE BHOYS SPILL THE BEANS

MOST fans would love to be a fly on the wall in the Celtic dressing room but we've come up with the next best thing. So just who is the biggest moaner, the best trainer or the worst dancer at Celtic Park? The only way to find out is by asking the only ones who know the true answers – the players themselves. So read on as some of your favourite Celtic heroes spill the beans on some of your favourite Celtic heroes.

P.S. – there are some more revelations on pages 56/57.

SCOTT BROWN

Most skilful?

Aiden McGeady. Some of the stuff the wee man does with a ball is frightening. He's an unbelievable talent.

Best trainer?

That's a hard one, but I'd have to say Barry Robson. He gets stuck in and gives his all every day.

Biggest moaner?

Scott McDonald. All the boys would say that. Wee Scotty isn't happy unless he is moaning.

Worst dancer?

Gary Caldwell thinks he can move but his dancing is absolutely shocking – the worst I've ever seen.

Worst taste in music?

That's an easy one – Evander Sno's music is unbelievably bad. It's just rubbish.

Biggest joker?

Chris Killen likes a joke and you always have to watch yourself when he's lurking in the shadows.

Worst dress sense?

Gary Caldwell again. Some of the stuff he wears to training is shocking. I think he gets dressed in the dark.

Most intelligent?

There are a few bright boys, but Steven Pressley was an intelligent big guy, or he thought he was!

JOHN KENNEDY

Most skilful?

Who do you think? There is only one answer to that question – Aiden McGeady.

Best trainer?

Darren O'Dea always puts in a good shift out on the training pitch. He's a really hard worker.

Biggest moaner?

I'm sure I'm not the only one who will say Scott McDonald. Some days he's worse than others, but he just loves a moan.

Worst dancer?

Stephen McManus. His dance moves are shocking but for some reason, he thinks he can groove on a night out. He's terrible.

Worst taste in music?

That would have to be big Mick McManus again. I've been in his car a million times and the stuff he listens to is horrific…he listens to country music.

Biggest joker?

Scott Brown and Chris Killen are a bit of a double act. They play jokes on each other but they also team up and you have to be on your guard.

Worst dress sense?

Again, I'm sure I'm not the only one who will say Gary Caldwell. You just have to take a look at the clothes he wears to training.

Most intelligent?

This is a hard one, because there are a few intelligent boys about, but Steven Pressley had a sensible head on him.

STEPHEN McMANUS

Most skilful?

It would have to be Aiden McGeady. I've played with him for a long time and some of the stuff he does with a ball is mind-blowing.

Best trainer?

All the lads work hard to be fair. There is nobody who doesn't pull their weight – the manager wouldn't allow it.

Biggest moaner?

I'm a bit of a moaner myself, but Scott McDonald can moan with the best of them when things don't go his own way.

Worst dancer?

Gary Caldwell. If we have a team night out, Gaz thinks he can give us some moves, but he looks ridiculous.

Worst taste in music?

Take your pick from a lot of the boys, but whenever I think about dodgy music, the name Evander Sno comes to mind. His stuff is shocking.

Biggest joker?

Scott Brown. He's always hyper and always has to be up to something as well. He's come up with a few crackers over the last year.

Worst dress sense?

I could slag off a few of the boys here, but some of Steven Pressley's gear was rank rotten. He was once voted one of the most stylish men in Scotland as well – that's unbelievable.

Most intelligent?

Aiden McGeady is really intelligent. Before he joined Celtic full-time, he did his exams and got really good marks in his Highers.

BARRY ROBSON

Most skilful?

Aiden McGeady. I've played with him and against him and he's a phenomenal talent. You never know where he's going to go or what he's going to do.

Best trainer?

Myself! Just kidding, all the boys give their all in training and it would be unfair to pick one out. In fact, I'm just going to say myself after all!

Biggest moaner?

There's nothing wrong with moaning in football and at Celtic, Scott McDonald is the King of the Moaners.

Worst dancer?

There are a few that I could name and shame, but Gary Caldwell can't dance to save himself. He's really poor.

Worst taste in music?

Once again, there are a few boys with questionable tastes in music, but Mr Caldwell again takes the prize as having the worst.

Biggest joker?

We've got a young squad, so you always need to be on your toes and Aiden McGeady comes up with some good stuff.

Worst dress sense?

All the young lads think they have the trendy gear, but most of it is shocking. Aiden McGeady has the worst.

Most intelligent?

There can only be one answer. This is a guy whose intelligence shines through on and off the park – myself!

THE NUMBERS GAME

THERE are magic numbers, lucky numbers, favourite numbers and something that we always hope the opposition is doing – making up the numbers.

Certain numbers have become synonymous with particular Celts and specific eras in the club's history.

Here are just some of Celtic's favourite numbers.

1 is the position Celtic finished in the SPL last season. The Champions pulled off one of the most dramatic league triumphs in the club's history when they finished top of the table once again after clinching the title on the last day.

3 is for the trio of SPL titles won by Celtic in the last three years. When he guided Celtic to his third successive title last season, Gordon Strachan made history by becoming only the third manager to do so. Willie Maley and Jock Stein are the other managers.

7 was the number worn by Celtic legends Jimmy Johnstone and Henrik Larsson when they played for the club. The number has now become synonymous with Celtic and the club also has the No.7 restaurant inside Celtic Park.

9 is the record amount of Scottish League titles won

in succession by Celtic between 1966 and 1974. Managed by Jock Stein, Celtic also won the European Cup during the most successful period in the club's history.

31 was the amount of goals scored by Scott McDonald in his debut season with Celtic. The Australian finished as the top scorer in Scotland with that impressive tally.

46 is the shirt number worn by Celtic winger Aiden McGeady. The 22-year-old, Scotland's current Player of the Year, wore that number on his Celtic debut in 2004 and has never changed it.

67 Celtic made history in 1967 when they beat Inter Milan 2-1 in Lisbon to lift the European Cup. Managed by Jock Stein, the Celtic team, now known as the Lisbon Lions, was: Simpson, Craig, Gemmell, Murdoch, McNeill, Clark, Johnstone, Wallace, Chalmers, Auld and Lennox.

88 Celtic Football Club played their first-ever match on May 28, 1888. The opponents were Rangers and the final score was 5-2 to Celtic. The scorer of the club's first ever goal was Neil McCallum.

71 stands for the score in one of the most famous wins in the club's history, which was Celtic 7, Rangers 1. The game took place at Hampden on October 19, 1957 and remains Celtic's biggest win over their city rivals.

100 Celtic Football Club turned 100 years old in 1988 and celebrated by winning the Scottish Premier League and Scottish Cup double. Billy McNeill was the manager during one of the best seasons in Celtic's history.

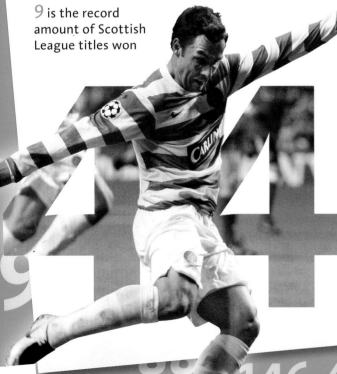

468 is the number of goals Celtic's all-time top scorer Jimmy McGrory scored for the club. Second on the list of top scorers is Lisbon Lion Bobby Lennox with 273 goals, while Henrik Larsson scored 242 goals and is third on the list.

790 is the record amount of games that Billy McNeill, captain of the Lisbon Lions, played for Celtic, between 1957 and 1975. Cesar, as he was known to his team-mates, also managed Celtic on two separate occasions and enjoyed great success.

80,000 is the estimated number of supporters who travelled to Seville in Spain to see Celtic take on FC Porto in the 2003 UEFA Cup final. The Portuguese side won 3-2.

146,433 was the attendance when Celtic beat Aberdeen 2-1 in the 1937 Scottish Cup final at Hampden. The crowd remains a European record for a club match.

1,017,894 is the number of supporters who watched Celtic play in the SPL at Celtic Park during season 2007/08. The actual capacity of Celtic Park is 60,506.

PLAY FOR CELTIC

At every home game there are 60,000 people wishing they could be one of the 11 Bhoys on the pitch – thanks to the club's community programme, some of the younger fans, including YOU, might just fulfil that dream

HOW would you like to live the ultimate dream of playing for Celtic and running out at Paradise in front of 60,000 adoring fans?

Thanks to Celtic in the Community's Play for Celtic programme, it could be a lot easier than you think and the door is open to all.

The Play for Celtic programme enables youngsters aged from 5 to 13-years-old to 'Live the Dream' and play for Celtic in recognised leagues throughout Scotland.

The initiative is aimed at players of all abilities, and the club are also on the look-out for talented players to advance into the Centre of Excellence programme or the Celtic Youth Academy itself.

This exciting and challenging programme gives young players the opportunity to receive carefully structured weekly coaching sessions providing the 'ultimate football experience' for any young player.

Youngsters also have the opportunity to pull on the famous Hoops and play for Celtic every week against other boys' clubs in local development associations across the country.

The programme is a fantastic new way to get a foot on the ladder, as well as an opportunity to play regular small-sided games against other centres.

If, during training and in the games a player shows potential, he'll be invited to join a Centre of Excellence . . . and who knows?

The next step could be an invitation to join one of Celtic's seven Development Centres situated throughout Scotland.

There is also a similar programme for the girls and the club now operates a successful grassroots programme in addition to running teams from Under-11 to Under-17, as well as reserve and first teams in the Scottish Women's Premier League.

Everybody has to start somewhere and, you never know, it could be YOU.

As one graduate from the Celtic Youth Academy, a certain Aiden McGeady said: "Don't miss out on this great opportunity to Play for Celtic and receive excellent coaching from the Community Academy coaches, good luck and who knows maybe one day you could be running out in front of 60,000 Celtic fans."

Check out the Celtic Player Pathway to find out where it could lead you.

To find out more about the Celtic Foundation and its programmes contact Hazel on: 0871 226 1888 (option 5) or 0141 551 4321 – 9am to 5pm (Mon to Fri), email hwilson@celticfc.co.uk

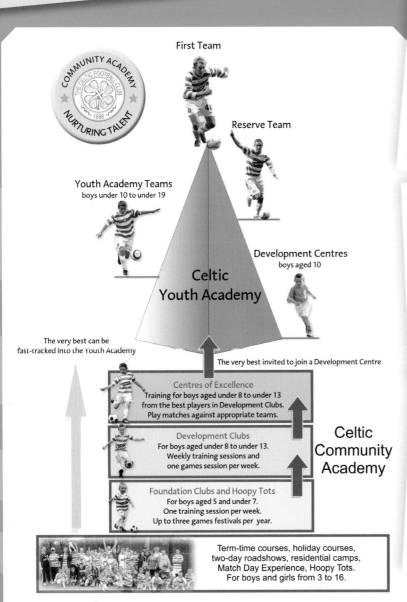

First Team

COMMUNITY ACADEMY
THE CELTIC FOOTBALL CLUB
1888
NURTURING TALENT

Reserve Team

Youth Academy Teams
boys under 10 to under 19

Development Centres
boys aged 10

Celtic
Youth Academy

The very best can be fast-tracked into the Youth Academy

The very best invited to join a Development Centre

Centres of Excellence
Training for boys aged under 8 to under 13 from the best players in Development Clubs. Play matches against appropriate teams.

Celtic
Community
Academy

Development Clubs
For boys aged under 8 to under 13. Weekly training sessions and one games session per week.

Foundation Clubs and Hoopy Tots
For boys aged 5 and under 7. One training session per week. Up to three games festivals per year.

Term-time courses, holiday courses, two-day roadshows, residential camps, Match Day Experience, Hoopy Tots For boys and girls from 3 to 16.

DOT-TO-DOT

Join up all the dots in this picture and see if you can identify the Celtic star who played a major part in the final league game of the victorious campaign.

* Indicates new line start (Answer on pages 60/61).

EUROPEAN QUESTION TIME

01   Who did Celtic play in the UEFA Champions League qualifiers last season?

02   And what was significant about the away venue?

03   Who scored Celtic's goal that night?

04   In the home tie, Artur Boruc's crucial winning penalty save was against which player?

05   What UEFA Champions League group were the Bhoys in?

06   Who scored Celtic's first goal in the group stage?

07   And who scored the Hoops' last goal in the group stage?

08   Which young Hoop played at Celtic Park for the first time ever when Barcelona visited?

09   And which player was he marking?

10   Which Celt opened the scoring that night?

Check out the answers on pages 60/61.

Did you know...

When Neilly Mochan signed in 1953, his first four games were played at Hampden - meaning he had picked up two medals (Coronation Cup and Charity Cup), played in front of 292,160 fans and scored four goals before he even played at Celtic Park!

THE BHOYS SPILL THE BEANS

SOME more eye-openers as your Celtic Annual reveals the secrets of the Hoops dressing room.

Can you see any patterns emerging here in the fame and shame departments?

GARY CALDWELL

Most skilful?

That's easy. Aiden McGeady is one of the most talented players I've ever seen in my life.

Best trainer?

All the boys put in a good shift out on the training pitch, so it would probably be unfair to pick one out, although Barry Robson gives his all.

Biggest moaner?

Aiden McGeady likes a moan from time to time if he's not happy with the way things are going, but there's nothing wrong with that.

Worst dancer?

That's a tricky one because I've seen the boys trying to dance, but I'd have to pick Lee Naylor. He's pretty bad.

Worst taste in music?

Evander Sno's music is horrendous. I don't know how he can listen to it.

Biggest joker?

Chris Killen is always up to something. It doesn't matter where or when, he's always up to something.

Worst dress sense?

Scott Brown's gear is horrific. He thinks he looks the business, but he hasn't got any taste.

Most intelligent?

Steven Pressley was a clever big guy and always had something to say about what was going on in the world.

PAUL CADDIS

Most skilful?

Aiden McGeady – there's no contest. He's amazing with the ball at his feet.

Best trainer?

Barry Robson is a bit of a beast on the training pitch and hates losing. He gives it everything.

Biggest moaner?

Scotty McDonald loves a moan in training and on the pitch. There are a few others, but he's the biggest moaner.

Worst dancer?

I honestly couldn't say for sure, but I've heard that Gary Caldwell isn't the best of dancers.

Worst taste in music?

Most of the boys like the same stuff, but Evander Sno always listens to this weird music on his iPod. It's brutal.

Biggest joker?

Scott Brown likes a practical joke. He's always throwing something or hiding stuff about the place.

Worst dress sense?

Gary Caldwell gets some abuse for his clothes and it's not hard to see why, to be honest with you.

Most intelligent?

I'm not really sure who I would say from the current squad, but Steven Pressley was a really intelligent big guy.

DARREN O'DEA

Most skilful?

I was going to pick a centre-half, just because I am one, but I'd have to be serious and say Aiden McGeady. He's one of the most talented players I've ever seen.

Best trainer?

Mark Brown, the goalkeeper, is one of the best trainers at the club. He's a fit lad and he always keeps himself sharp by doing some extra work.

Biggest moaner?

I think you can probably tell from watching games, but Scott McDonald loves moaning. He just loves it.

Worst dancer?

Gary Caldwell is pretty bad, but Bairdy (Alan Baird) the masseur is one of the worst dancers I have ever seen in my life. He's horrendous.

Worst taste in music?

Evander Sno. He probably has the worst taste in music of anyone I have ever met in my life. I can't begin to say how bad it is.

Biggest joker?

Scott Brown and Chris Killen are the double act to look out for. They are always up to something, no matter where we are.

Worst dress sense?

As well as his dancing, Gary Caldwell has a strange taste in clothes. I don't even know where to start with him – it's all wrong.

Most intelligent?

Big Steven Pressley always struck me as being a really intelligent guy. The rest of the boys…I'm not too sure.

MARK WILSON

Most skilful?

There are a few candidates, but Aiden McGeady is pretty much out on his own in terms of skill.

Best trainer?

That's a hard one, because all the boys try to put in a good shift. If I had to pick one, I'd say Darren O'Dea. He always works hard.

Biggest moaner?

Scott McDonald – without a doubt. If there is another answer given to that question, I'd be stunned.

Worst dancer?

I don't really know to be honest. If you watched the title celebrations last season, you'll see that most of the boys can't dance.

Worst taste in music?

Some boys like to think they are into their music and some of the stuff isn't bad, but Evander Sno has to be nailed for his music.

Biggest joker?

A few people like to play the odd joke now and then but I'd probably say that Aiden McGeady is the biggest joker of the lot.

Worst dress sense?

There's one man way ahead in this category and that's Gary Caldwell. The reasons are self-explanatory.

Most intelligent?

Of the current squad, it's hard to say, but Steven Pressley always came across as being quite intelligent.

THE origins of the Celtic Huddle can be traced all the way back to the small northern German town of Jheringsfehn. Former Hoops defender Tony Mowbray is credited as the man who started it all on July 23, 1995, before a friendly match with German side Kickers Emden. Celtic lost the pre-season friendly 2-0.

TONY MOWBRAY wanted to start the Celtic Huddle as a show of togetherness by the players. Years later, he said: "Every player likes to leave something that people can remember them by and maybe the Huddle is mine at Celtic. I'm delighted to see it still going strong, because it's been a brilliant way of uniting the players and the fans. It's in the fabric of Celtic now."

THE first 11 players to take part in the Celtic Huddle were: Pat Bonner, Lee Martin, Malky Mackay, Tony Mowbray, Tosh McKinlay, Rudi Vata, Peter Grant, John Collins, Pierre van Hooijdonk, Andy Walker and Brian McLaughlin.

ANDY WALKER can vividly remember the first-ever Celtic Huddle pep-talk delivered by Tony Mowbray and said: "The Huddle grew beyond all our expectations and we made it clear that, while none of us would be at the club forever, it was important that any newcomer would be told that this was a special part of being a Celtic player."

THE 11 players to take part in the first-ever Celtic Huddle at Celtic Park, before a 1-1 draw with Newcastle United on August 5, 1995, were: Gordon Marshall, Mark McNally, Tony Mowbray, Tom Boyd, Tosh McKinlay, Rudi Vata, Peter Grant, John Collins, Phil O'Donnell, Pierre van Hooijdonk and Andy Thom.

JOHN COLLINS, another original member of the Celtic Huddle, is stunned at the impact it had on the club. He said: "We were looking for something to bring us together, to give us a bit of final bonding. Some of the lads were a bit shy about it, especially as it was so public, but it just grew from there."

SINCE it was created in 1995 to the start of this season, it's estimated that the Celtic Huddle has been performed in 31 countries by the Hoops first-team, before friendlies and competitive matches. Those countries are: Scotland, England, Ireland, Wales, Spain, Italy, France, Germany, Portugal, Georgia, Lithuania, Switzerland, Luxembourg, Austria, Holland, Ukraine, Russia, Poland, Sweden, Slovakia, Finland, Croatia, Israel, Norway, Denmark, Belgium, Hungary, Czech Republic, USA, Canada and Japan.

AT the end of last season, the Celtic Huddle had been performed before 678 competitive games at home and abroad since 1995. That means over 30 MILLION football supporters will have witnessed the stunning sight of the Celtic Huddle.

THE one and only Henrik Larsson holds the record for appearing in the most Celtic Huddles before competitive games. The Swedish legend took part in 312 Huddles during his Celtic career. Jackie McNamara is in second place with 307 appearances, while Neil Lennon took part in the Huddle 300 times. Honourable mentions should also go to Paul Lambert (253) and Stilian Petrov (245). From the first generation of Huddlers, Tom Boyd appeared in it most with a total of 238 appearances.

CURRENT Celtic captain Stephen McManus grew up watching his heroes perform the Huddle and is honoured to now lead the side into it before every game. He said: "All the players and supporters love the Huddle and it really gets us fired up before the games. We are all proud to continue the strong tradition of the Celtic Huddle and will continue to do so."

CELTIC'S mascot Hoopy the Huddle Hound takes his name from the Celtic Huddle…many Hoops fans were also members of the World Huddle Club. In addition, Celtic TV's flagship programme is called the Daily Huddle.

CELTIC teams from all age groups now perform the Celtic Huddle before games. Perhaps the biggest Huddle ever witnessed on the pitch was after Celtic won the league at Tannadice at the end of last season.

QUIZ ANSWERS:

SPOT THE DIFFERENCE (Page 20)

SPL SEASON 2007/08 CHAMPIONSHIP QUIZ ANSWERS (Page 21)

01   Kilmarnock, in a 0-0 draw.

02   It was Kenny Milne of Falkirk with an own goal.

03   Gretna.

04   Scott McDonald and Aiden McGeady.

05   Four - Hearts, St Mirren, Inverness and Aberdeen.

06   19.

07   Five.

08   33.

09   Stephen McManus with 37.

10   Ryan Conroy, Jim O'Brien, Paul Caddis and Paul McGowan.

WORDSEARCH ANSWERS (Page 27)

01.   Lennoxtown

02.   Tannadice

03.   ScottMcDonald

04.   Paradise

05.   Southampton

06.   Netherlands

07.   Champions

08.   JockStein

09.   TheHuddle

10.   EuropeanCup

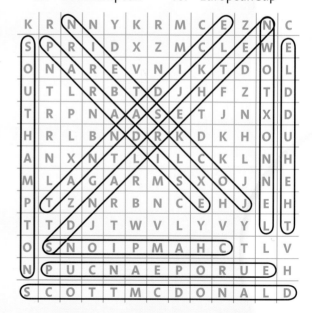

QUIZ ANSWERS
(Page 27)

01. 42 times.
02. Andreas Hinkel.
03. Georgios Samaras.
04. Four, twice each against Motherwell and Gretna.
05. Three, Willie Maley, Jock Stein and Gordon Strachan.

MAZE (Page 26)

See opposite

GUESS WHO?
ANSWERS (Page 47)

01. Aiden McGeady
02. Barry Robson
03. Ben Hutchinson
04. Paul Hartley
05. Scott McDonald
06. Stephen McManus

DOT-TO-DOT
ANSWER (Page 54)

Jan Vennegoor of Hesselink
(see opposite)

EURO QUIZ
ANSWERS (Page 55)

01. Spartak Moscow.
02. The Luzhniki Stadium was also used for the final.
03. Paul Hartley.
04. Maxim Kalinichenko.
05. Group D.
06. Stephen McManus against AC Milan.
07. Massimo Donati in the 90th minute against Shakhtar Donetsk.
08. Paul Caddis.
09. Ronaldinho.
10. Jan Vennegoor of Hesselink.

CHAMPIONSHIP CELEBRATION